Charlie Oatway was born in 1973 and grew up in the Shepherd's Bush area of west London. He left school at the age of thirteen and became a footballer, first with Wimbledon, then non-league Yeading, before getting his first professional contract with Cardiff City. After being sent to prison for GBH, he played for Torquay and Brentford before joining Brighton and Hove Albion in 1999, captaining them, and winning two championships and three promotions.

After injury ended his career, Charlie worked for Albion in the Community (AITC) as a manager of community relations and a leader of their award-winning adult learning initiatives. He is now the club's first-team coach.

All proceeds from this book will be donated to Albion in the Community. For more information see www.albioninthecommunity.org.uk

D1317056

Tackling Life

The true story of a footballing
bad lad made good

Charlie Oatway

CORGI BOOKS

TRANSWORLD PUBLISHERS
61–63 Uxbridge Road, London W5 5SA
A Random House Group Company
www.rbooks.co.uk

TACKLING LIFE
A CORGI BOOK: 9780552161787

First publication in Great Britain
Corgi edition published 2011

This book is a work of non-fiction based on the experiences and
recollections of the author. The author has stated to the publishers
that the contents of this book are true.

A CIP catalogue record for this book
is available from the British Library.

Addresses for Random House Group Ltd companies outside the UK
can be found at: www.randomhouse.co.uk
The Random House Group Reg. No. 954009

The Random House Group Limited supports The Forest Stewardship
Council (FSC), the leading international forest certification
organization. All our titles that are printed on Greenpeace approved
FSC certified paper carry the FSC logo. Our paper procurement
policy can be found at www.rbooks.co.uk/environment

Typeset in 12/16pt Stone Serif by
Kestrel Data, Exeter, Devon.
Printed in the UK by
Cox & Wyman, Reading, RG1 8EX.

2 4 6 8 10 9 7 5 3 1

Mixed Sources
Product group from well-managed
forests and other controlled sources
www.fsc.org   Cert no. TT-COC-2139
© 1996 Forest Stewardship Council
FSC

Acknowledgements

I would like to thank the following people who have helped me in their own way to get me where I am today.

To begin with I thank Ritchie Jacobs from back home who got me into the pro game in the first place. Then the next biggest influence was Micky Adams who signed me for Brighton and Hove Albion. Then following on from Micky I want to thank all of the directors at the club, and in particular Dick Knight, Martin Perry, Derek Chapman, Ken Brown, Tony Bloom (Mr Chairman) and his brother Darren. Also a special mention to Paul Camillin, the Albion's Press Officer, who has managed to get me through a couple of scapes! All of these people have been so supportive to me over my career.

I thank my wife and kids who have been through all of the ups and downs together with me.

Finally I would like to thank Alan Sanders who has helped me to write this book, and we had so much fun doing it. He pushed me to focus on my literacy and numeracy skills and also helped me to achieve all of my football qualifications. He has been like a mentor to me and has led me through the difficult times.

For everyone else you are either mentioned in the book, or you'll be in the next one!

Tackling Life

Chapter One

Pentonville Prison

To me, the summons for a court case in London on a Monday morning in 1994 was not a major problem. How could I have known at the time that it was to be the worst moment in my life? You see, I was playing professional football for Cardiff City at the time, and although I had been charged with GBH I was reliably informed (or so I thought) by my brief, that the most I would get was community service or a fine.

I had played for Cardiff on the Saturday, and after the game I told the manager, Terry Yorath, that I had to go to court in London the following Monday. I said that I would be back for training on the Tuesday. I explained that when I was living in London before I'd signed for Cardiff, I had got involved in a fight when my mate, who is Afro-Caribbean, was racially abused. We both piled in, won the fight and didn't think much more of it. Unfortunately the police did, and if I didn't go to London they would come and arrest me at the training ground.

Terry was brilliant and promised that he and the club would do all they could to keep it out of the papers. He said that he would see me on the Tuesday when I got back. I was so confident that I would be back in a few days that I told my wife, Sonya, to stay in Cardiff and not to bother travelling with me.

The train down to London was a good time for me to relax. I had only been at Cardiff for two months and in some ways I had become a local hero. I had been playing well and my face had been plastered on the side of local buses to advertise something or other.

Even when the judge said my full name, 'Anthony Phillip David Terry Frank Donald Stanley Gerry Gordon Steven James Oatway, you are sentenced to six months imprisonment', I still wasn't too worried. This was because he went on to say, 'It will be reduced by one month as it's your first offence, and another month for helping with the police inquiries.'

I was sure he would continue to reel off the

months and let me go, or finish by saying that it was a suspended sentence. Instead, he finished by saying, 'I hereby sentence you to four months imprisonment. Take him down.' I was then handcuffed by the two policemen on either side of me and they led me downstairs to a cell and slammed the door.

My mind was racing. They told me I was in a holding cell, and that they would have to ring round the prisons to find out where I would be staying. I had so many things going on inside my head.

For a start I was angry that my mate who I had stuck up for in the fight didn't turn up at court to tell them what had happened. Sonya, my wife, had tried to get hold of him, and when she did he said he'd got the dates mixed up and couldn't make it. My mate went on to play for QPR (Queens Park Rangers) and I suppose he didn't want anything to get in the way of his chance of becoming a professional footballer.

I also felt cheated because, not only did he not turn up, but also there were no witnesses in court and everything was just read out from statements.

I felt very hard done by as my close family

friend Dennis Wise had just been let off a six-month prison sentence for GBH towards a taxi driver. If a high-profile footballer like him could be let off, why couldn't I?

I was now really worried about which prison they would send me to. I was hoping it would be Wormwood Scrubs as I knew a few people in there who could make sure I was all right. I was also worried about Sonya and wondered how she'd cope with it all. I knew I had really let her down and that she didn't deserve any of this.

People have asked me since whether I was worried about being beaten up or abused by other prisoners, but that was never a concern of mine. I would fight any man if I had to. I had too many other things to worry about, like what would happen to my football career? I had only just made it and now I seemed to have blown it.

After what felt like three or four hours they told me I would be going to Pentonville and not the Scrubs as I had hoped. I still have vivid memories of being put inside the police van. There were other prisoners in there, but everyone was squashed into tiny compartments where there was no room at all. You can see out into the street through a small window but no one can see you. I remember all the noise in the van on the way to Pentonville. The journey only lasted about an hour, but it felt a lot longer as the other prisoners were banging and shouting all the way there.

When we arrived I was led through the gates into the reception area, and once I'd been given my prison uniform, I was interviewed. Things didn't get any better then because when I told the officer that I was a professional footballer he didn't believe me. 'Well, that's a first,' he said. 'I've had people tell me they are the Prime Minister but never a professional footballer.'

A few hours later, the prison officer who had interviewed me told me he was also a goal-keeping coach and had worked with Terry Yorath when he was at Swansea. He had done some checking up on me and apologised for not believing that I was a footballer. He then promised he would look after me and make sure I stayed fit for when I got out. This was my first glimmer of hope. He also told me that although I had been sentenced to four months, I would be out in two if I behaved myself.

In many ways I was lucky. I was put in a cell

with a Rastafarian who I got on well with and the prison officer who'd interviewed me kept his word and made sure I got the best jobs. The other prison officers were blunt but never rude to me, so there was no problem there, but I struggled with panic attacks and the feeling that I couldn't cope for the first few days.

It wasn't long before I was taken to another cell, which I would share with an armed robber. I got on well with him but the thing that helped me the most was a visit from my uncle Terry. He had been in prison many times and said he'd do anything to put himself behind bars rather than see me suffering. He also gave me a reality check, saying, 'You're only in there for a shit, shower and shave, then you'll be out.'

In fact this was the message I got from most of the prisoners I spoke to. They said that as I was only in prison for such a short time, I shouldn't worry about it. Some of them were serving up to twenty years, so I couldn't really expect any sympathy from them, not that I wanted any.

Prison was horrible. There were lots of things that made me depressed. When I was first led into prison, the sight of dead cockroaches lying on the ground outside really got to me. I couldn't cope with the fact that the only topic of conversation in prison seemed to be about the length of time people had to serve. What was I doing in this place?

The jobs I was given included being on reception helping to hand out prison clothes to newcomers, boxing up their own clothes and taking them down to the stores. A plus point of this job was that I was able to spend long periods of time outside my cell, which was a much better deal than most of the prisoners got. It also meant that while I was there I was able to meet every prisoner who arrived. As I was the one to give them their supplies, it meant that in some sense I was doing something for them, and because of that I pretty much got on with everyone. Those who didn't have jobs, which was about 80 per cent of the prisoners, had to spend long periods of time banged up inside a cell. This, in my opinion, is no good for them or anyone else.

As prisons are full of criminals, lots of bad stuff goes on in there. I never really saw much violence myself, although there were one or two nasty incidents. One man was sliced across the face with a broken dinner tray for pushing in the food queue. Even for someone like me who had been in a few fights, that shook me but also made me realise the tension and danger that comes with prison life.

The other incident was far more serious. As I was only sentenced for a short time, and because I got on with everyone, most of the inmates seemed to want to keep me out of trouble. It is commonly known that when a 'nonce' (someone who has been found guilty of committing a sex crime, usually with children) comes into a prison, the other prisoners try to beat them up any time they can. When it happened this time, some of the prisoners made sure I was sent on a wild-goose chase to get me out of the way while they gave the nonce a good hiding.

I only found out what had happened when I got back from the made-up job, which meant I was completely in the clear. I was glad they had kept me out of the way so that no one could point the finger at me. It just shows you what a dangerous place prison can be.

After a month my appeal came up, which could have gone any of three ways. If I lost the appeal I could have been given a longer sentence, or I might have had to start the sentence again. On the other hand, I could have been found not guilty, in which case I'd be let out straight away.

Quite simply, I was not prepared to take the risk of the first two outcomes, so I cancelled the appeal. I would rather keep my head down and just serve the remaining month. To me it was an easy choice.

When the day finally came for me to be released, I was allowed to leave at 7 in the morning, which is unusual as prisoners are normally let out at about 11 o'clock. This was because I got on well with the prison officers and they said they would let me go first thing. Leaving prison did not make me feel brilliant. Instead, I just felt numb from the whole experience, which had really shaken me and changed my whole outlook on life.

When I was younger and often in trouble, the thought of prison didn't worry me. Many of my relatives and friends had been there at some point, and I thought it was a likely place for me to end up. Now it had happened to me, I knew that I had to avoid prison at all costs. I had tasted the good life as a professional footballer. I knew that I was never ever going back to prison.

Chapter Two

'The Bush'

I suppose in a way, whether I liked it or not, from the minute I was born my life was always going to be different to that of most people.

It didn't help that my dad decided to have a £50 bet with a friend that he would name me after the eleven members of the Queens Park Rangers first team. Thanks, Dad! What an idiot. So why was I called Charlie? Well, when my aunt came to the hospital to visit my mum and me, she said that I looked more like 'a right little Charlie'. My mum and everyone else agreed, so that's the way it stayed. Still, as long as you won the £50 bet, Dad!

When I think about it, the local police probably thought it was my dad, Tony, who was the right little Charlie, although they might have used something a bit stronger to describe him. He was a 'totter' (a scrap-metal merchant), who topped up his income by stealing. As a result, he's spent half his life in prison. He and his brother George were both sent to borstal at the age of twelve, where they spent two years, so not exactly a great start.

Having said that, it must have been difficult for both of them when they were growing up. Their dad (my grandfather) had spent most of his adult life either in the army or in prison. So many of my dad's and uncle's teenage years were spent trying to look after their sisters as well as my grandmother, who was ill with cancer for a couple of years.

We had a massive family network in and around Shepherd's Bush in west London. That was a rough neighbourhood in those days. Everyone I met growing up in 'the Bush', as we called it, seemed to be related to us and was introduced as a 'cousin' or 'uncle'. The family was full of colourful characters and the Oatway name seemed well known. My dad Tony and Uncle George were both successful boxers in their teens. As I was growing up, my dad got me interested in all sports, which meant staying up late to watch everything on TV from darts to test cricket.

My dad wasn't too strict, but he wouldn't let us get away with much in the house (when he was there). He never hit us; shouting would do the trick because I didn't like to cross him. He tried to point me in the right direction away from the police and was keen to show me that prison should be avoided.

Dad had no favourites in our family, but he was very keen for me to visit him in prison. It wasn't just so we could stay in regular contact, but also, I think, he wanted me to see, at an early age, that prison wasn't a nice place to be. Prison was to my dad what Fletcher from the TV series *Porridge* called 'an occupational hazard'. It was just part of his life of crime.

It was quite common to see someone I knew, or was related to, in prison. I remember hearing some of my relations moaning to one another at a family gathering years later that one of my aunts wasn't 'one of us' because none of her children had been to prison!

Deep down I think my dad accepted that if anyone from our family was going to get into trouble it would probably be me. The youngest of the family with two older brothers and two older sisters, I was more mouthy than the others. I would often get caught fighting at school or getting into trouble some other way.

Thinking back, I have a lot of sympathy for my mum, Doreen. She worked hard as the manageress of a local Curtis shoe shop, as well as trying to keep the family together when my dad was in prison. She was from a tough working-class background in west London and was used to hard work, but I doubt she'd been expecting this kind of lifestyle.

When I was about eight or nine, I was taken to football matches by my dad and one of my older brothers, Roy. My home was in Loftus Road, the first house next to the Queens Park Rangers (QPR) football stadium. I would often climb over the fence to watch the match with my brothers and cousins. Our dog stood guard and tried to ward off anyone trying to do the same. We were worried that if too many people got in for free they'd get caught and we would be stopped.

Throughout the hard times, family loyalty kept us together. I remember my dad giving money to family, friends or neighbours who had just come out of prison to help them get back on their feet. Everyone pulled together and my family got the same help when my dad was in prison.

We lived in a big council house and we always had cousins staying with us, normally because one parent was in prison. We got on well with our visitors and there were never any problems between us. We were raided by the police a few times, too, but I don't remember them ever finding any of the stolen goods they were looking for.

My brother Roy, who is eight years older than me, has always been really supportive throughout my life, particularly when I was younger. He worked really hard at school and got good qualifications. When he left home he moved out of 'the Bush' and went into banking, where he's had a good career ever since.

Despite the differences in our lives and characters, Roy has remained close to me. He regularly drove miles after work to give me reading and writing lessons, as well as driving me to football training and matches.

My other brother Barry, who is ten years older than me and a qualified gas fitter, was just as supportive. He always looked after me when it came to money and clothes. He also got in the odd fight for me when I got into trouble.

I remember once when I was about ten, I was with my family in the Old Oak Club in East Acton and I was up to my usual trick of annoying people. This time it was a girl. When her brother came over to tell me off, Barry stepped in to help me. I could see that Barry was getting more and more upset as the two got into a heated argument. I tried to stand in between them, but wasn't able to stop them trading punches.

I was in the middle, about twelve inches smaller than the two of them, trying to hold Barry back. It's an image I'll never forget and one of my earliest memories of feeling guilty. Whoops! Perhaps I shouldn't have started that.

Living in 'the Bush' in terraced houses that led straight out onto the pavement helped us get to know our neighbours. In some cases this was good because it helped create a close-knit community. Many of the local parents would sit on their doorsteps and chat to their neighbours while their kids played football in the streets. Some people didn't think this was such a great idea, though, because their cars would get hit by the footballs and they'd come out on the street ranting and raving.

For me, between the ages of seven and twelve, having people sitting out on the streets was a great chance to earn some money. I became quite good at break-dancing and family and friends would pay £1 each to watch me perform. My friend Andy Colbert and I used to go to clubs like the Old Oak in Acton and earn money by break-dancing on the dance floor. That was a nice little earner.

Whatever I did, there was always trouble round the corner. I regularly got into fights, and because I was small, I lost as many as I won. I remember one fight when I was eleven against a boy who scratched me quite badly all over my face. When I got home I was surprised to find that my family were more worried about whether or not I'd won than how I was. A lot of the time I was told I had to join in fights even though I wasn't that keen.

As I got a bit older, I progressed from being a bad fighter to an even worse crook. My first failure was at thirteen when two friends and I decided to mug the 'tally man'. The 'tally man' used to come around to people's houses to trade, buying and selling clothes, offering loans and so on. We knew that he always carried money, most of which would have been taken from our neighbours to repay their loans. We planned to steal this cash and give it back to them, like young Robin Hoods.

My friends Richard and Spencer and I waited for three hours for the 'tally man' to come by, but he never showed up. We were freezing cold and in the end we gave up. Sadly for us, he had been delayed, and ten minutes after we got home there was a knock on the door. There we were in our black clothes, still trying to take off the shoe polish we'd put on our faces as a disguise. I'm sure that having seen us in this state he knew what we'd been planning, but, instead of robbing him, our families ended up paying over the money we owed him.

It was around this time that Richard thought of another great chance for earning some money. It involved going to a parade of shops near Victoria Station in central London. The plan was that we'd do the simple task of smashing the shop windows and grabbing some expensive cameras. Unfortunately, we weren't strong enough to break the glass as we didn't realise it was reinforced. Before we knew it the police had turned up. There was a helicopter overhead and we got caught. Richard went straight on remand, as he was older than me, but I was let off with a caution.

My dad was disappointed with me on two counts. First, for getting involved in crime despite his warnings, and second (and perhaps more importantly, for him) for failing. He must have felt I was dragging the family name through the gutter by being such a bad criminal, and after everything he'd done to build his reputation. To be fair, I didn't want to get involved in crime: I was just easily led. Older boys only took me along because I was under age and could take the blame. Well, that's my story anyway.

Now and then my troubles spilt over into family life. When I was fourteen and my brother Barry was out, I 'borrowed' his car. I stopped at a zebra crossing to let a woman walk across the road, and I couldn't believe my bad luck when she looked through the windscreen to see who was driving. It wouldn't have mattered but it was my Aunt Rita!

I drove a few miles away and ditched the car, but by this time Aunt Rita had told Barry, who was on the warpath and out looking for me. Before long, everyone in the local area seemed to have heard about the incident. Barry eventually caught up with me and gave me a real hiding. It was probably because my aunt had told him I was a better driver than him because I stopped for people at zebra crossings!

Chapter Three

Acting the Fool at School

When I look back at my early years growing up, life was quite hectic. I was the youngest of a family with five kids and there were always people coming to visit. Some of them were welcome whilst others, like the police, weren't.

Like any kid going to school for the first time, I was a bit nervous, but I soon got into the swing of things. I went to Miles Coverdale School in Shepherd's Bush and I have very happy memories of when I first started. I got on well with the teachers and the other kids, and I was learning new things all the time.

Between the ages of five and eight, I enjoyed school and had no idea that I had a problem with reading and writing which would affect my whole life. At the time, I didn't think I was different to anyone else. Most of the writing I remember doing was copying off the board, and for some strange reason I quite enjoyed that. It wasn't until I was about nine that I began to realise a lot of the other children in my class were getting ahead of me with their lessons. I noticed it most when we were asked to write our own stories. I could make them up all right in my head, but I couldn't get them down on paper. My spelling was all over the place and it took me so long to write anything that I pretty much lost interest.

While I may not have been doing well in the classroom I was achieving something outside of it. I was playing a lot of football with other boys who lived on my estate and I found I had a bit of a talent for it. I suppose playing with lads who were older than me helped. I was smaller than them, but I soon learned how to make sure this didn't stop me from being one of the best. People have asked me since whether I liked playing other sports, but I was only interested in football, football, football.

There was a guy called Les who worked for QPR and he used to come and do an after-school club with us. There was no school football team, but I knew by the time I was eight that I was as good as any of the eleven-year-olds I was play-ing with. The school sent me for trials for the West London District team and I got in. I also played for Harrow Boys Club and the Bedfont Eagles.

The manager of the Eagles used to come all the way over from Bedfont, pick me up for the games and then drive me home again after-wards. The round-trip must have been at least twenty miles. Knowing that someone was pre-pared to do that for me, even though I was still at primary school, certainly made me feel good about myself.

When I look back, the football was a great education for me in itself. All the kids I played with, and those from my school, came from different racial backgrounds. Not that it mattered to any of us as we all learned to get along just by playing football together. The colour of people's skin was never an issue.

But with my dad constantly in and out of prison, life was hard for my mum. She not only had to raise us but also hold down a full-time job at the shoe shop. I'm not sure if people coming in and out of our house daily, to visit or to stay, made her life any more difficult, but she managed to look after us well.

Although my football was going from strength to strength, everything inside the classroom seemed to be going wrong for me. As my frustration with reading and writing grew, so my behaviour got worse. The teachers started to take me out of the classroom when I misbehaved and I soon decided that this was the best option. When I was sent outside into the corridor to work, I couldn't be made to look stupid in front of the other kids. For me the corridor was a comfort zone, and if it meant misbehaving to get there, so be it.

Of course all of this came at a cost. I wasn't learning anything, but that wasn't the thing that worried me at the time. What really got to me was that because I played up, I was never allowed to go on school trips. I remember crying and pleading with the teachers to let me go, but the answer was always no.

I have to admit that it wouldn't be right to put all of my misbehaviour down to my struggles with reading and writing. I enjoyed being a tearaway. Quite a few members of my family, and the people I hung around with, were tearaways too. I suppose it just goes to show that you're either born into that role or you fall into it.

On one occasion a friend and I broke into a log cabin on the school playing field where all the PE equipment was kept. We didn't want to steal anything, we just thought it would be fun to break in. The head teacher went mad and made us stand up in assembly while he told everybody what we'd done. I was so embarrassed I cried. The school also told my mum, and I got a right telling off as soon as I got home as well.

By the time I finished at primary school, I had a reputation not only for being badly behaved but for struggling with the work. To be honest, I think the staff at Miles Coverdale were glad to get rid of me, and I suppose I can't blame them.

Like most of the kids from my primary school I went on to Burlington Danes secondary school in Wood Lane, Shepherd's Bush, which just happens to be next to Wormwood Scrubs Prison. At least visiting any of my relations when they got put away in there didn't involve a long journey!

A few weeks before I left Miles Coverdale, a

couple of teachers from Burlington Danes came to visit us at home. They said they'd read all the reports about me and seen samples of my work. They didn't think there would be a problem when I started at secondary school. The teachers said that although I might be a bit behind most of the other kids, it wouldn't take me long to catch up. My mum was delighted and so was I. It gave me the lift I needed and I felt I had the chance of a new start and that this time I wasn't going to blow it.

Sadly, though, it wasn't to be. I was nervous, but there was also the added pressure that I would get found out again. I was worried that the teachers would discover I was terrible at reading and writing.

It didn't take long for me to realise that I just couldn't do the work. First I decided that the easiest way out was to copy someone else, but that didn't solve anything, so I just went back to the only solution I knew: I started messing about. I got into a lot of trouble with the teachers for general misbehaviour, but I didn't get into fights with the other kids.

My form teacher wasn't much help either. She was an Australian who was only in England for a year and she spent most of the time telling us she couldn't wait to get back home.

The final straw came when I fell out with one of my teachers over reading. I completely lost it, picked up a chair and threw it at him. From then on there was no way back. I got booted out of school having only lasted one term of the second year.

The education authorities decided that I should go to Wood Lane Special School, but I knew from the minute I walked into the place that I didn't belong there. All the other kids had either physical disabilities (quite a few were in wheelchairs or had cerebral palsy) or had mental health issues. Even though I was young, I knew that the problems they had, which I felt really sorry about, were not the same as my problems with learning. The staff offered to pick me up in the blue school bus, but I said I'd rather walk. The truth was I didn't want to be seen in a school bus for children with problems.

The school itself was right next to Burlington Danes, so while I was there I took care not to be seen by any of the kids from my old school, and when it was break time I avoided going into the playground.

My behaviour at this second new school was really good, but because I wasn't actually ill they told me I had to leave and go to a place called a 'Projects Special Unit'. This is a place for children with serious behaviour problems and there was no way my mum would let me go there.

Mum said that this school was a breeding ground for criminals, and I think to a certain extent she was right. She fought the local authority tooth and nail to stop me from being sent there, but they refused to give in. For my mum there was only one solution: I would have to stay at home. So from the age of thirteen I didn't go to school again.

My brother Roy came down on a weekly basis to help me with my reading and writing as my mum couldn't afford a tutor, but I never took any exams. If I'm honest, life away from school was a bit boring. I had one friend who used to wait until his parents had gone to work, then bunk off school and come round to my place, but we didn't really get up to much. I spent my time watching daytime television and waiting for the other kids to get out of school. Then we'd go on to the Suttons Estate in Notting Hill to play and hang around.

When I look back I know I let myself down, but I can't help thinking that the authorities let me down, too. I don't think this sort of thing would happen nowadays, but I may be wrong.

Chapter Four

Bad Lad on the Streets

People have often asked me what I got up to when I was hanging around. Well, for one thing I never smoked or took drugs. None of that appealed to me, and to be honest it wasn't something many of my mates got into either. I did drink a bit, but not much more than most fourteen- or fifteen-year-olds. We just wanted to have a laugh, and we messed about, mostly at each other's expense. I have to admit there were a few activities we shouldn't have been involved in, though, like breaking and entering and fighting.

At fourteen, I was very grateful when my brother-in-law's dad offered me a job selling fish tanks at a shop in east London. A lot of kids who were thrown out of school worked there from time to time and we all earned £50 a week.

I used to give the money to my mum so that she could keep it and give it back to me when I needed it.

When I was fifteen, I got a job with my cousin Warren in a warehouse in Notting Hill doing painting and decorating, but by this time my football was beginning to take off in quite a big way. A school in Holland Park called Cardinal Vaughan allowed me to play for them, even though I'd never even been to the school. Slightly corrupt I know, but I wasn't complaining. If anyone ever asked me why I didn't go to school, I used to say I was a bad kid and no school would have me, which I suppose was basically true.

Two of the people who helped me most with my football career in the early days were my cousin Terry Oatway and a player called Wally Downes. They were the best of mates and used to hang around together. Wally played semi-professionally for Wimbledon and was also on the coaching staff there, so he and Terry arranged for me to have a trial. After that, the club agreed to let me train there for a month. My football impressed them so they got me to sign some schoolboy forms, which for someone who wasn't attending school seemed a bit strange!

Life at Wimbledon went well, although one of the coaches seemed to have a problem with me. It all started while we were on a pre-season trip to Sweden. One time I arrived back from a night out two hours after curfew. Although there were a few of us, he picked on me rather than anyone else, claiming I was the ringleader.

When we got back to England, he took it upon himself to look into my background, and the more digging he did, the worse it got for me. He found out that there had been an incident with a taxi driver when a few of us did a runner after getting a cab back to the estate. We'd paid some of the bill but didn't have enough money to pay the full amount. The cab driver went ballistic and said he'd come back with some other drivers to sort it out, which he did. There was a bit of a fight and the police were called.

For some reason they picked on me and shoved me in a van, then they drove me to the police station. They were a bit over the top when they took me out of the van and bundled me into the cell, and one of them kicked me in the head. Then they put white forensic overalls on me. When my brief arrived, I told him what had happened, and although the police denied it, my brief noticed some blood on my overalls, which could only have come from my head. The police decided to drop all charges because they knew they could get into serious trouble, and in the end I was cleared.

But that didn't stop the coach from finding out about it, and he started asking me all sorts of questions. There was nothing that bad to find out, though my friends and I were involved in 'borrowing' a few cars from local garage showrooms (I'll never understand why they always left the keys in the cars!). For the record, we never damaged any of them and just used to leave them in a nearby road.

Although a couple of my friends got in trouble with the police over that, I was never caught, so the coach could only go on hearsay. That, however, didn't stop him making sure I was seen as the 'bad boy' of the youth team. The year I joined the team, 1988, was when Wimbledon were at their peak, with a reputation for having a few 'lively' players, like Vinnie Jones, Dennis Wise and John Fashanu, so in a way I fitted in quite well.

At the end of the 1989/90 season, when I was sixteen, the club decided to let me go rather than sign me as a trainee. It was a blow because I'd really thought I had a chance of going on to the next stage. Instead, I signed for a non-league club, Yeading, at semi-pro level and had a really good pre-season.

A scout for Derby County saw me play and asked me up there for a week's trial. Things went well and at the end of the week they said they'd be back in touch. The trouble was they kept dithering and wouldn't make up their minds. Yeading spoke to them and said they ought to let me know one way or another, but I told Yeading to tell them to forget it and I decided to stay with them instead.

Football aside, I was getting involved in some petty crime, mainly a bit of stealing here and there. I also had a job labouring and gardening, which mainly consisted of helping to build brick walls at the fronts and backs of people's gardens. What with that and my earnings from Yeading I was bringing in enough to get by.

Meanwhile my personal life had got a bit complicated. I'd been going out with a girl called Debbie since I was about thirteen, and when I was seventeen we had a son we called 'Charlie boy'. Debbie was from an Irish Catholic background, so an abortion was out of the question. We were lucky, though, because once she had Charlie boy, we jumped the council waiting list and got a flat in Loftus Road.

Things were going OK, but we were both too young to settle down and looking back it was never going to work. I'm no angel, but did she have a temper! I thought at times she must be a bit mad, though I guess she must have been to hook up with me in the first place.

It was when we had one of our major bust-ups that I met my wife, Sonya. I'd been separated from Debbie for a couple of months but thought we would probably get back together. Then a friend of mine arranged a blind date with his girlfriend's mate. The four of us went to a do at Yeading Football Club, funnily enough, and Sonya and I hit it off straight away. We didn't see each other for a week as the next day I was off on a pre-season tour, but when I got back we started going out. Within three months Sonya became pregnant with Talia, so by the age of nineteen I had two children with two different mothers.

It was then that I started to think I should be a bit more responsible. Sonya was eighteen and had a pretty good job with a decent wage and a company car working for British Airways in the finance department. Considering where I'd come from, I'd done pretty well to be with someone who had such a good job.

The 1993/94 season with Yeading went really well and the football team got promoted. There were quite a few clubs looking at me, but they always seemed to come to the same conclusion: that I was too small to play in central midfield at a professional level.

At the end of that season a guy called Ritchie Jacobs, who was a community worker on the estate, somehow got me and a couple of my mates, Joe Omigie and Alan Mills, a trial at Cardiff City. I was the only one of the three of us who was invited back after the week's trial, although Joe went on to play for Brentford.

I have to say at this point what a good bloke Ritchie was to set this up for us. He could see that we were three young lads with some talent, who were pretty much wasting our lives and needed a break, and he set up the trial out of the goodness of his heart.

During the week's trial, I realised that the professionals we were training with were really no better than me. That started to build my hopes up, although in the back of my mind I was still preparing for another failure. When Cardiff asked me back for another month, I knew it was the chance I'd been waiting for, and I was going to grab it with both hands.

Chapter Five

Making it, and Nearly Breaking it

When I arrived at Cardiff City Football Club in the summer of 1994, life was good. I had been given a one-year contract, which was an incredible feeling. I was confident that I had the ability, as long as I could remain free of injuries and stay out of trouble.

I knew from experience how my life might turn out if I didn't make this work, and I was determined to stay in professional football. What I didn't know was that for the next few years my life was going to be all about survival and overcoming some major hurdles.

I was on £200 a week and I really had no expenses. I was given digs on Barry Island in the Majestic Holiday Camp. This was owned by the club chairman, Rick Wright, who'd taken it over from Butlin's in the 1980s. It was a bit strange being in the same complex as holidaymakers, but I didn't mind. I was only in there for two weeks before I was moved to a pub so I could be nearer the training ground. Finally I settled into a bed and breakfast that was owned by the manager's step-daughter and her husband. This was good because they could keep an eye on me and I couldn't get away with anything, even if I wanted to.

I settled in well at Cardiff and loved it there. I got on with the other players, most of whom were Welsh, but there were a few English players as well as a couple from Ireland. Every Friday we'd have small games with the Welsh playing the English. The tackles used to fly in, and to be quite honest some of them were horrendous. We got quite a bit of rain that summer and autumn, so the tackles were made even worse due to the slippery surface.

Of course there was lots of banter that went along with this and the manager, Eddie May, allowed it all to happen. I remember thinking that although I loved it, it didn't really seem like the right thing to be doing. There were quite a few occasions when players couldn't play on the

Saturday because they'd been injured in a Friday game.

I couldn't believe my luck. I was playing in the first team and everyone at the club treated me really well. It seemed that wherever I went in Cardiff, people knew me. I was offered massive discounts whenever I went shopping and I generally got the best of everything. I wasn't just recognised in Cardiff either. I remember going into the Welsh valleys for a drink one evening and being spotted by some Swansea supporters. I didn't hang around for long. Anyone who knows about the rivalry between Cardiff and Swansea will tell you there is serious hatred between them.

With everything going so well, the last thing I wanted was my past catching up with me, so as you can imagine, the two months I spent in Pentonville Prison were a bombshell I can't put into words.

That spell inside was a true test of character for me, but it wasn't just being in prison that I was worried about, I was also concerned about the reaction of my team-mates when I got out. I shouldn't have worried, though, because on my first day back it was as if I'd never been away.

They asked me what it was like inside prison and then we got straight on with the football. It was almost as if they were asking me what I'd done over the weekend.

As for worrying about the reception I would get from the Cardiff fans, I needn't have bothered about that either. I wasn't fit enough to play in the first game after my release, so instead I was taken out to the centre of the pitch before the game where I was given a standing ovation. I think the fact that my offence was GBH meant it was almost seen as part of football culture. Not that I feel proud of what I did, but I do think that sticking up for a friend while he is being racially abused isn't the worst crime in the world.

Some big changes had taken place at the club while I was in prison. By the time I was released there had been a change in both the owners and the management at Cardiff. Eddie May had been sacked and the new owners, the Kumar brothers, instructed the new manager, Kenny Hibbitt, to put me out on loan to another club.

I was sent to Coleraine in Northern Ireland. I actually preferred this to playing in the reserves at Cardiff, although the standard was way below what I was used to. All the players were part-time and the pitches weren't the best either. I was getting my full-time wages, but to be honest I wasn't that comfortable there.

Being English didn't help. Had it not been for Paul Millar, who was a fellow ex-professional at Cardiff now playing for nearby club Linfield, I would really have struggled. Our wives got on very well, so when Sonya moved out to join me it was just about bearable. I have to say that living in Northern Ireland was quite a steep learning curve. There seemed to be no police around, just the army, and there were loads of sealed-off areas, none of which was my cup of tea.

When I returned to Cardiff, I played in the reserves until the end of the season, when we were relegated to Division 4. Fortunately though, the club decided to give me another one-year contract. I've heard a lot of people in professional football say that one of the hardest things is to get an extension after your first year, so at least I'd managed to do that. The problem was I still wasn't in the first team.

One day I was playing in the reserves in an away match against Torquay, whose first-team manager happened to be my ex-boss at Cardiff, Eddie May. He asked me if I would consider a transfer, which was music to my ears. I moved down to Torquay before Christmas and went straight into the first team, and although I only played for half the season, I still managed to be awarded 'player of the year'.

That was the good news, but the bad news was that we finished bottom of the league. Fortunately for us, the champions of the Conference (the league below the main Football League), Stevenage Borough Football Club, were unable to make the ground improvements necessary for promotion, so we were saved.

At the end of the season, Eddie moved to manage Brentford and Torquay brought in Kevin Hodges. The change in management didn't have a big effect on our results, though, because they couldn't attract players to Torquay. It was a long way from anywhere and there was little chance of scouts coming to see us play, although I suppose there were always the away games. Playing away meant travelling hundreds of miles and we didn't have the money for many overnight stays.

You may think that being a professional footballer is glamorous, but it didn't feel like it then, not that I was moaning. I remember travelling by coach on a Sunday to play Hartlepool on the Tuesday. By the time we got back in the early hours of the Wednesday morning my little boy Charlie was going to school. I felt as if I had jet lag and I hadn't even left England.

One thing I was beginning to realise was that I really loved the battle of the game. In some ways it didn't matter to me that we had to scrap for every point as I was in my element. I think that's why I won player of the year the previous season: I just ran, tackled and battled for the whole ninety minutes. A nil-nil away from home was cause for celebration in my book.

I think my past may have helped me with this never-say-die attitude. I felt that playing professional football was such a fantastic thing to be doing and running around a football pitch was no hardship at all. I see a lot of lads playing today who have more talent than I ever had, but they don't have a chance in hell of making it because they don't want it enough. They lose concentration too easily and don't have that will to win.

I only lasted a few months into the 1997/98 season at Torquay before Brentford put in an offer for me. The wrangling between the clubs went on for what seemed like ages before the deal was done. When it was finally sorted I was really pleased to make the move, not least because the club was in London. Eddie May was the manager and they were playing in the division above Torquay, having just missed out on promotion to the Championship.

I have to give a quick mention to Eddie May at this point as I owe him such a lot. Over a period of three years he took me from Cardiff to Torquay and then on to Brentford. If it hadn't been for him, my professional career might have been a lot shorter. Eddie always believed in me, and as so often happens in football, when a manager moves clubs he buys players who have played under him before.

Eddie used to make me laugh. He managed like he had played: he used to be a big centre half and he took no prisoners. He would get so mad when he was manager. His mind worked quicker than his mouth, so when he tried to say something he couldn't speak quickly enough. He couldn't even swear properly!

When I arrived at Brentford, life wasn't all a bed of roses. Dave Webb was the chairman

Quick Reads 📖

Books in the Quick Reads series

Quick Reads 📖

Great stories, great writers, great entertainment

Bloody Valentine

James Patterson

Arrow

This year Valentine's Day isn't for romance.
It's for murder

Mega-rich restaurant owner Jack Barnes and his second wife Zee are very much in love. However, their plans for Valentine's Day are about to be torn apart by the most violent murder. Who is the strange figure plotting this sick crime? Who hates Jack that much? There are plenty of suspects living in Jack's fancy block of flats. Is it them, or could it be the work of an outsider with a twisted mind? One thing's for sure, the police have got their work cut out solving this bloody mess.

This gory murder mystery will make you feel weak at the knees.

Quick Reads 📖

Great stories, great writers, great entertainment

Strangers on the 16:02

Priya Basil

Black Swan

A very ordinary train journey goes horribly wrong

It's a hot, crowded train. Helen Summer is on her way to see her sister Jill and tell her an awful secret. Another passenger, Kerm, is on his way back from his grandfather's funeral. They are strangers, jammed against each other in a crowded carriage. Noisy school kids fill the train – and three of them are about to cause a whole heap of trouble. In the chaos, Helen and Kerm are thrown together in a way they never expected. Catching a train? Read *Strangers on the 16:02* and you'll never feel the same way about your fellow passengers again.

Quick Reads 📖

Great stories, great writers, great entertainment

Trouble on the Heath

Terry Jones

Accent Press

A comedy of Russian gangsters, town planners
and a dog called Dennis

Martin Thomas is not happy. The view he loves is about
to be blocked by an ugly building. He decides to take
action and organises a protest. Then things go badly
wrong and Martin finds himself running for his life. Along
the way he gets mixed up with depressed town
planners, violent gangsters and a kidnapped concert
pianist. Martin starts to wonder if objecting to the
building was such a good idea when he finds himself
upside down with a gun in his mouth.

This hilarious story from Monty Python star, Terry Jones,
will make you laugh out loud.

Quick Reads 📖

Great stories, great writers, great entertainment

Quick Reads are brilliantly written short new books by bestselling authors and celebrities. Whether you're an avid reader who wants a quick fix or haven't picked up a book since school, sit back, relax and let Quick Reads inspire you.

We would like to thank all our partners in the Quick Reads project for their help and support:

Arts Council England
The Department for Business, Innovation and Skills
NIACE
unionlearn
National Book Tokens
The Reading Agency
National Literacy Trust
Welsh Books Council
Basic Skills Cymru, Welsh Assembly Government
The Big Plus Scotland
DELNI
NALA

Quick Reads would also like to thank the Department for Business, Innovation and Skills; Arts Council England and World Book Day for their sponsorship and NIACE for their outreach work.

Quick Reads is a World Book Day initiative.
www.quickreads.org.uk   www.worldbookday.com

Other resources

Enjoy this book? Find out about all the others from
www.quickreads.org.uk

Free courses are available for anyone who wants to
develop their skills. You can attend the courses in your
local area. If you'd like to find out more, phone
0800 66 0800.

For more information on developing your basic skills in
Scotland, call The Big Plus free on 0808 100 1080 or visit
www.thebigplus.com

Join the Reading Agency's Six Book Challenge at
www.sixbookchallenge.org.uk

Publishers Barrington Stoke (www.barringtonstoke.co.uk)
and New Island (www.newisland.ie) also provide books
for new readers.

The BBC runs an adult basic skills campaign.
See www.bbc.co.uk/raw.

www.worldbookday.com